How Is a Building Like a Termite Mound?

Structures Imitating Nature

Walt Brody

Lerner Publications • Minneapolis

Lerner Publications Company
An imprint of Lerner Publishing Group, Inc.
241 First Avenue North
Minneapolis, MN 55401 USA

For reading levels and more information, look up this title at www.lernerbooks.com.

Main body text set in Billy Infant regular.
Typeface provided by SparkType.

Editor: Brianna Kaiser

Library of Congress Cataloging-in-Publication Data

Names: Brody, Walt, 1978- author.
Title: How is a building like a termite mound? : structures imitating nature / Walt Brody.
Description: Minneapolis : Lerner Publications, [2022] | Series: Lightning bolt books - imitating nature | Includes bibliographical references and index. | Audience: Ages 6-9 | Audience: Grades 2-3 | Summary: "Animals build unique and beautiful homes. So do humans. But sometimes human-made buildings harm the environment. Learn how architects use biomimicry to design eco-friendly buildings"— Provided by publisher.
Identifiers: LCCN 2020009482 (print) | LCCN 2020009483 (ebook) | ISBN 9781728404172 (library binding) | ISBN 9781728418414 (ebook)
Subjects: LCSH: Architecture and biology—Juvenile literature. | Sustainable architecture—Juvenile literature. | Biomimicry—Juvenile literature.
Classification: LCC NA2543.B56 B76 2022 (print) | LCC NA2543.B56 (ebook) | DDC 720/.47—dc23

LC record available at https://lccn.loc.gov/2020009482
LC ebook record available at https://lccn.loc.gov/2020009483

Manufactured in the United States of America
1-48475-48989-11/6/2020

Table of Contents

Inventions from Nature

Architects design buildings. They improve old building designs too. These designs make people's lives easier.

Architects make drawings of buildings. These drawings are called blueprints.

Architects sometimes get design ideas from nature. This is called biomimicry. *Bio* means "living," and *mimic* means "to copy."

A Termite Mound

Zimbabwe is a hot country in Africa. Architects need to design buildings that are cool. But cooling buildings uses a lot of energy.

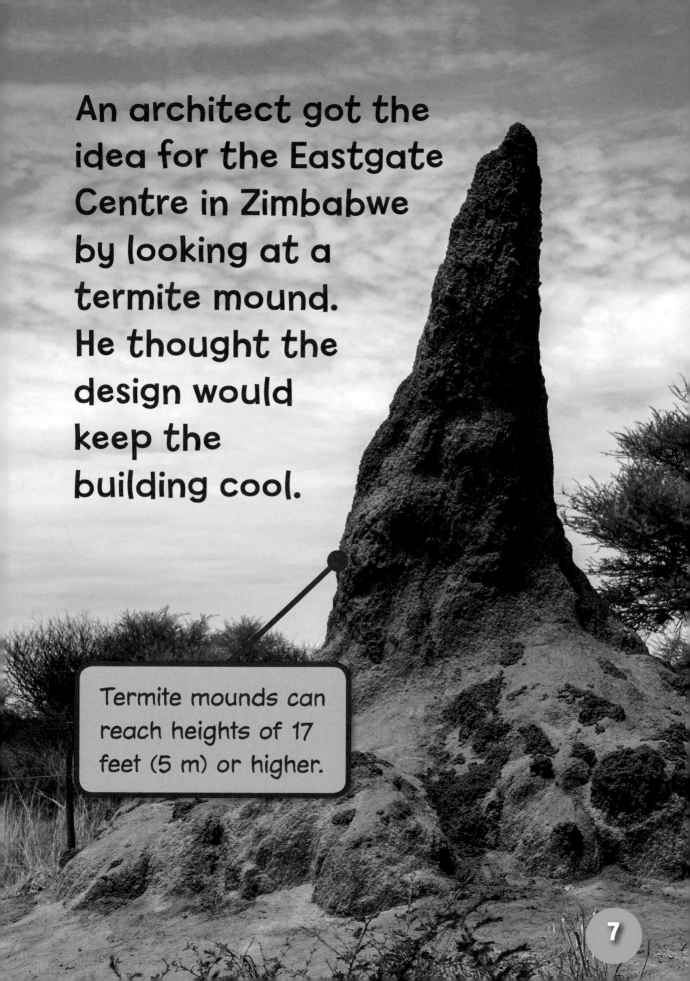

An architect got the idea for the Eastgate Centre in Zimbabwe by looking at a termite mound. He thought the design would keep the building cool.

Termite mounds can reach heights of 17 feet (5 m) or higher.

Termites live underground. They build a mound over their home. This mound works like a chimney. It pushes hot air out and cools their home.

Termite mounds are made up of soil, termite saliva, and termite poop.

The Eastgate Centre

The Eastgate Centre has tunnels that wind flows through. The concrete walls absorb heat, but the wind pushes the heat out.

A Sea Sponge

The Gherkin is a building in London, England. It got its name because it looks like a gherkin, a fruit used for making pickles.

The Gherkin's architects looked to the ocean for building ideas. They copied a sea sponge for the design of the Gherkin.

Architects can find design ideas even at deep depths of the ocean.

The Venus' flower basket sea sponge lives in the ocean near the Philippines. Its exoskeleton is good at letting water flow through it.

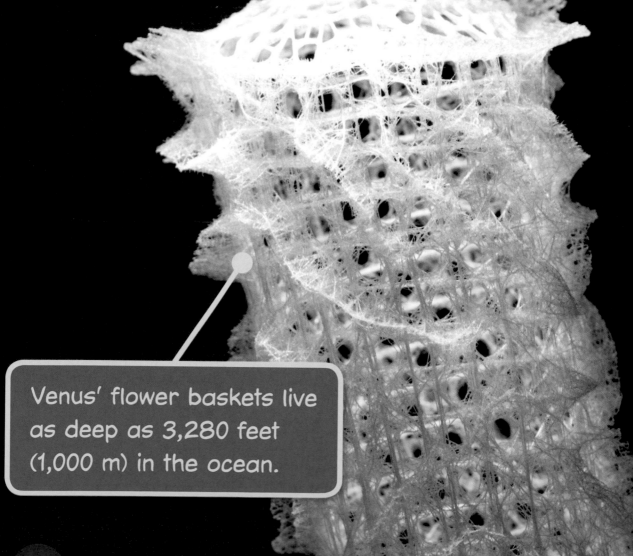

Venus' flower baskets live as deep as 3,280 feet (1,000 m) in the ocean.

The Gherkin's structure is designed to act like the Venus' flower basket's exoskeleton. This lets air flow through it.

The Gherkin's structure is like the sponge's exoskeleton. It helps give the building good airflow. This keeps the building cool and lowers energy costs.

The Durian Fruit

Singapore is in Southeast Asia. One building there is designed to look like a fruit. The building is the Esplanade theater.

Durians are covered in spikes.

The durian fruit in Asia is grapefruit-sized and has a spiky husk. It is famous because it has a strong smell.

Like the durian fruit, the Esplanade theater is covered with spikes. The spikes help shade the building.

The Esplanade theater close up

The theater's spikes move. They follow the sun throughout the day. This keeps the building in the shade. The building stays cooler.

Growing Bricks

Bricks are used for many types of buildings. Bricks are made in a very hot kiln. Heating the kiln uses a lot of energy.

But the company bioMason makes bricks at room temperature with sand and bacteria.

It takes three to five days to make a bioMason brick.

The company makes some bricks from waste products. These bricks can save a lot of energy. This is good for the environment.

The Future of Building

Buildings use a lot of energy. Scientists look to nature for new ways to save energy. Rose butterflies might help. They live in Southeast Asia. Their black wings absorb light easily. Scientists are trying to find out how the butterflies do this. Better light absorption could make solar panels better. Solar panels make electricity from the sun's rays.

Glossary

architect: someone who designs buildings

bacteria: very small, single-celled life-forms

biomimicry: getting ideas for inventions from nature

exoskeleton: the outer structure that supports and protects an animal's body

husk: the tough outer skin of some fruits

kiln: a very hot oven used to harden bricks and pottery

mound: hill or pile

waste product: an unwanted or unusable material

Learn More

Brody, Walt. *How Is a Ship Like a Shark? Vehicles Imitating Nature*. Minneapolis: Lerner Publications, 2022.

Generation Genius
https://www.generationgenius.com/videolessons/inspired-by-nature-biomimicry-video-for-kids/

Hirsch, Rebecca E. *Climate Change and Energy Technology*. Minneapolis: Lerner Publications, 2019.

Kiddle: Architecture Facts for Kids
https://kids.kiddle.co/Architecture

Swanson, Jennifer. *Beastly Bionics: Rad Robots, Brilliant Biomimicry, and Incredible Inventions Inspired by Nature*. Washington DC: National Geographic, 2020.

Index

Photo Acknowledgments

Image credits: Mangostar/Shutterstock.com, p. 4; almqje/Shutterstock.com, p. 5; Tawanda Kapikinyu/Shutterstock.com, p. 6; Bildagentur Zoonar GmbH/Shutterstock.com, p. 7; Kittiphoto/Shutterstock.com, p. 8; Thomas Cockrem/Alamy Stock Photo, p. 9; Donatas Dabravolskas/Shutterstock.com, p. 10; Aleksei Alekhin/Shutterstock.com, p. 11; Arctium Lappa/Shutterstock.com, p. 12; PeskyMonkey/Shutterstock.com, p. 13; ZDL/Shutterstock.com, p. 14; Benny Gunawan Slamet/Shutterstock.com, p. 15; Lim Neng Du/Shutterstock.com, p. 16; Jerome Quek/Shutterstock.com, p. 17; mathefoto/Shutterstock.com, p. 18; Alastair Wallace/Shutterstock.com, p. 19; Aisyaqilumaranas/Shutterstock.com, p. 20.

Cover Images: Art Konovalov/Shutterstock.com; Viacheslav Lopatin/Shutterstock.com.